The Life of
Roald
Dahl

A Marvellous Adventure

The Life of Roald Dahl

A Marvellous Adventure

by Emma Fischel

Illustrations by Martin Remphry

W
FRANKLIN WATTS
LONDON•SYDNEY

Franklin Watts
First published in Great Britain in 2016
by The Watts Publishing Group

3

Copyright © text Emma Fischel, 1999
Copyright © illustrations Martin Remphrey, 1999

Credits
Series Editor: Sarah Ridley
Series Designer: Cathryn Gilbert
Consultant: David Wray and Dr Anne Millard

Dewey number 823/DAH
ISBN 978 1 4451 5159 5

Printed in Great Britain by Clays Ltd, St Ives plc

Franklin Watts An imprint of
Hachette Children's Group
Part of The Watts Publishing Group
Carmelite House
50 Victoria Embankment
London EC4Y 0DZ

An Hachette UK Company
www.hachette.co.uk
www.franklinwatts.co.uk

MIX
Paper from
responsible sources
FSC
www.fsc.org FSC® C104740

Roald Dahl

Roald Dahl is one of the most famous children's writers ever.

Even children who don't like reading very much like HIS books.

Roald knew exactly what children liked to read about and how to tell a story well.

That's why his books have sold millions of copies all over the world.

Every day letters from children and their teachers poured through his letter box. He tried to answer them all.

Both Roald's parents were Norwegian but his father ran away from Norway when he was quite young. "I shall seek my fortune abroad," he said.

By the time Roald was born his father had made lots of money. It was a good thing too, as his family was rather big.

Then sad times hit the family. Roald's father and one of his sisters died within months of each other.

The family moved to a smaller
house which Roald loved. When
he was six he went to his first
school – by tricycle. There
weren't many cars on the road
back then.

There was no television either, no videos and no cinema. But there WERE sweet shops.

Roald and his family spent exciting summers in Norway. It took four days to get there by train and boat.

WELCOME TO TJOME

Back at home, Roald's mother said, "Now you are nine, it's time you went away to school. English boarding schools are the best of all!"

Roald didn't think so, though.

At thirteen he went to another school but that was even worse. Younger boys had to be servants to older ones.

Roald didn't get on with many of the teachers – and they didn't get on with him. He didn't like the rules and refused to bully the small boys.

He was made captain of two sports teams but that still didn't make him popular.

Good at games but who knows what he's thinking!

Not all the teachers were bad, though.

At last school was over. "And now, to university," said his mother.

"Not likely!" said Roald. "I shall become a businessman and travel the world."

"We are sending you to Egypt," said one of his bosses two years later.

"Too dusty!" said Roald. "And I'd like some jungles, please."

In the end they sent him to East Africa.

October 1938
From SS. Mantola.
Dear Mama,
Two weeks to get here, never mind. It would have been five to China! I am learning swahili.
Love from Roald.

Roald reached Africa at last.
"So much to see," he said. "So
different from home!"

Good morning,
Mr Giraffe!

Now we see faraway countries on television but in those days people only knew what other places were like from books.

While Roald was in Africa war broke out between Britain and Germany.

"I shall fly fighter planes for Britain," he said. "Once I learn how!" Then he drove six hundred miles to join the airforce.

Enormous crocodile!

Roald loved learning to fly. He was twenty-three …

and so tall his head stuck out of the plane.

But before he could do any
fighting he had a terrible crash.

It took him six months to
recover – and he limped for the
rest of his life.

Now he was sent to Greece to fight. But he had never flown in a battle before and he hardly knew how to fly the kind of plane they gave him.

Roald had trained with sixteen people. Thirteen of them died in the war.

After two months Roald started
to get terrible headaches. He
couldn't fly properly any more.

"It's because of that crash," said
the doctors. "You're no use
to the airforce. Go home."

Before long he was sent to America as a sort of spy. He had only been there three days when he met someone who changed his life.

"I'm writing about the war for a magazine," said the man. "Tell me about your flying days."

"I can do better than that," said Roald. "I'll write it all down for you instead."

The next thing he knew, every word he had written was printed in the magazine!

After that Roald became a
writer but his first books were
for grown-ups.

He lived some of the time in
England, some in America.

It was in America that he met a
famous actress, Patricia Neal.
They married within a year
and bought a house in England.

They had five children, four girls and a boy. Roald used to tell them bedtime stories. Later, these stories would become his first children's books.

Roald was forty-five when his
first children's book was published.
Then three years later, his second.
They sold more and more …

… and more.

Not everyone liked his books as much as children did though. Not that Roald worried too much about that.

Besides, he had a lot more story ideas in his head.

But terrible things were happening in Roald's life then. A taxi ran into his son Theo's pram when he was only four months old.

"He needs lots of operations and he may not get better," said the doctors.

"He will get better!" said Roald.

DOCTOR, WRITER AND AEROPLANE MODELLER INVENT THE WADE-DAHL-TILL VALVE

Roald invented a special gadget to help Theo's head get better. It helped other people too.

But then Olivia, his oldest daughter, died of measles. She was only seven.

Soon after Patricia, his wife, had something called a stroke. It made her very ill.

"Two visits a week from us and lots of rest," said the doctors.

"No," said Roald. "People around her and lots to do!"

Roald made her try to get better every hour of the day. If he couldn't be there he made sure someone was.

In two years she was making films again.

When Roald was fifty-one he
went to Hollywood to write a
film script for an exciting action
movie in the famous James
Bond series.

Writing the James Bond film
was fun – but Roald never
really liked any of the films that
were made of his own books.

Back home Roald had a special
hut tucked away in the garden.
He did all his writing there.

At the start of every day he
would sharpen six pencils to use.
By the end of the day they
would all be blunt.

He spoke every sentence aloud
to see if it worked. If it didn't he
rubbed it out.

Sometimes he got stuck on what
should happen next in the book.
And unstuck when he was doing
something quite different.

When he was sixty-six his own
favourite book was published,
The BFG. It was an exciting story
all about a big friendly giant.

Quentin Blake, the illustrator,
made the BFG look a lot
like Roald.

By now every new book Roald wrote was a bestseller. *The BFG* was the first book to win Roald a prize, though.

"A prize chosen by children," he said. "Thank you very much!"

Roald's next book, *The Witches*, won his first prize from grown-ups.

He gave the prize money to a hospital for very ill children.

"I'm honoured," he said, "But the Children's Book Award means much more."

For the next six years Roald carried on writing. But he got very ill himself, with something called leukaemia.

In November 1990 he died.

More about Roald Dahl

Did you know?

Roald was an expert on lots of things — orchid-growing, fine wines and paintings. He loved antiques as well, and he and his son, Theo, opened an antique shop in 1983. They had so much furniture to restore for the shop that Roald had to drain his swimming pool so they had somewhere to put it all!

The Roald Dahl Children's Gallery

You can visit the Gallery at the Buckinghamshire County Museum in Aylesbury to experience Roald Dahl's world. See what it's like to be inside a giant peach, discover one of Willy Wonka's inventions or come face to face with the BFG.

The Roald Dahl Museum and Story Centre

The museum is located in Great Missenden, which is the village where Roald Dahl lived and wrote for 36 years. It contains over forty fun and fact-packed interactive displays. It also houses all of Roald Dahl's manuscripts, his letters and his "Ideas Books". Peek into Roald Dahl's original Writing Hut and sit in his Writing Chair. Check out his archive on touch-screen monitors or make up your own Gobblefunk words. You can also create your own stop-frame animated story. There are always free craft activities on offer, and

all sorts of workshops, events, and free storytelling sessions, which are run in the school holidays and at weekends.

Roald Dahl's Marvellous Children's Charity

Roald did a lot to help people when he was alive. After his death, the Roald Dahl Foundation was started by Roald's second wife, Felicity. In 2010, it changed its name and became Roald Dahl's Marvellous Children's Charity. Up until 2009, the charity helped children who have problems with reading. The charity also gave help to children with brain damage and blood diseases until 2013. Now, Roald Dahl's Marvellous Children's Charity helps to make life better for seriously ill children and young people in the UK.

The Roald Dahl Funny Prize
In 2008, Michael Rosen, another children's author, decided to create a prize for funny books because he felt that they are often forgotten when it comes to prizes. It was named the Roald Dahl Funny Prize because Roald Dahl was so good at writing funny books himself! It was the first prize of its kind. There were two categories:

The Funniest Book for Children
aged six and under, and The
Funniest Book for Children aged
seven to fourteen. The Roald Dahl
Funny Prize ran from 2008 to 2013.

Roald Dahl wrote some of the best-loved children's books in the world. Here are a few of them:

James and the Giant Peach

This was Roald's first children's book to be published. It tells the story of a young orphaned boy called James Trotter who lives with his horrible aunts: Sponge and Spiker. They treat him very badly. His life changes when he meets a mysterious old man who gives him tiny green things, which will bring magic and adventure if James follows his instructions. On his way home, James trips and spills the green things by an old peach tree. The next day, a huge peach has grown on the tree. One night James finds a hole in the peach and climbs inside to discover a group of strange creatures and that is where the adventures begin...

James and the Giant Peach was turned into a film in 1996.

Charlie and the Chocolate Factory

This book is thought to be Roald Dahl's best-known story. Meet Charlie Bucket who lives with his mother, his father and his four grandparents in a little wooden house near a great town with a chocolate factory. Charlie loves chocolate, but his family don't have much money so the only time he gets a chocolate bar is on his birthday. One day, Mr. Willy Wonka, the owner of the chocolate factory, decides to open the doors of his factory to five children and their relatives. To choose who will enter the factory, Mr. Wonka hides five golden tickets in the wrappers of his Wonka chocolate bars. By luck, Charlie finds some money to buy an extra bar. To his amazement, he finds a golden ticket and a wondrous world awaits...

Charlie and the Chocolate Factory

has been made into two films and a
musical.

The BFG

The BFG — or, to give him his full
name, the Big Friendly Giant —
is one of Roald Dahl's favourite
characters. He is the smallest of all
the giants but unlike them, he is
kind. He
catches
dreams
and

stores them up in his cavernous home, before sharing the good dreams with sleeping children. One night he meets Sophie, who lives in an orphanage. Sophie and the BFG become friends, but Sophie is soon put in danger by the sudden arrival of the Bloodbottler Giant... *The BFG* won the Federation of Children's Book Groups Award in 1982 and was made into an animated film in 1989.

Matilda

This is Roald's last long children's book. It tells the story of Matilda Wormwood who is only five years old, but is a genius. Unfortunately her parents are too stupid to even notice. When Matilda starts school, she meets the lovely Miss Honey, her teacher. But she also has to deal with the awful Miss Trunchbull, the headmistress who is mean and cruel to everyone, especially Miss Honey. But what Miss Trunchbull doesn't know is that Matilda has a trick or two up her sleeve... *Matilda* won the Children's Book Award soon after it was published in 1988. It was made into a film in 1996 and a musical in 2010.

Quiz

1. Where did Roald Dahl's parents come from?
   a. Norway
   b. Sweden
   c. Finland

2. How was Roald treated when he went to boarding school?
   a. Everyone was nice to him
   b. The other children ignored him
   c. The older boys treated him like a servant

3. How did Roald think up the stories for his children's books?
   a. By reading children's books
   b. By making up bedtime stories to tell his children
   c. By pretending to be a child

4. How did Roald react to his wife Patricia's illness?
   a. He followed the doctors' orders
   b. He didn't know what to do
   c. He made her do all sorts of exercises to help her get better

5. Where did Roald like to write his books?
   a. In a special hut tucked away in his garden
   b. In a study in his house
   c. In a big armchair in his living room

Important dates in Roald Dahl's lifetime and after

1916 - Roald is born in Cardiff, South Wales.

1921 - Roald's father and sister both fall ill and die.

1925 - Roald goes to boarding school.

1929 - Roald goes to Repton Public School.

1934 - Roald leaves school at the age of 18.

1938 - Roald goes to Africa to work for the oil company, Shell.

1939 - The Second World War breaks out. Roald joins the RAF.

1941 - After a plane crash, Roald returns to Britain. His doctors tell him he can't fly planes anymore.

1948 - Roald's first book for grown-ups is published.

1953 - Roald marries Patricia Neal.

1960 - Roald's son Theo's pram is hit by a taxi in New York.

1961 - Roald's first children's book, *James and the Giant Peach*, is published.

1962 - Olivia, Roald's oldest child, dies.

1964 - Roald's second children's book, *Charlie and the Chocolate Factory*, is published.

1965 - Roald's wife, Patricia, has a stroke.

1967 - Roald goes to Hollywood to write a James Bond film: *You Only Live Twice*.

1982 - Roald's own favourite book, *The BFG*, is published.

1983 - Roald wins awards for *The BFG* and *The Witches* (published in 1983). He divorces Patricia and marries Felicity d'Abreu.

1988 - Roald publishes his last long children's book, *Matilda*.

1989 - Roald wins an award for *Matilda*.

1990 - Roald dies.

1996 - The Roald Dahl Children's Gallery opens.

2005 - The Roald Dahl Museum and Story Centre opens.

2006 - The first Roald Dahl Day is celebrated around the world on 13 September.

2008 - The Roald Dahl Funny Prize is launched.

2012 - The inside of Roald Dahl's writing hut is moved to the Roald Dahl Museum.

2013 - The Roald Dahl Funny Prize ends.

2014 - 50th anniversary of the publication of *Charlie and the Chocolate Factory*.

2016 - Roald Dahl is celebrated around the world on the 100th anniversary of his birth.

If you enjoyed reading about Roald Dahl's life, why not try these biographies of History Heroes...

Christopher COLUMBUS

DAMIAN HARVEY
Illustrated by MIKE PHILLIPS

978 1 4451 3294 5 pb
978 1 4451 3295 2 ebook

L.S LOWRY

DAMIAN HARVEY
Illustrated by TED SCANNA

978 1 4451 3308 9 pb
978 1 4451 3305 8 ebook

Neil ARMSTRONG

DAMIAN HARVEY
Illustrated by MIKE PHILLIPS

978 1 4451 3298 3 pb
978 1 4451 3299 0 ebook

Pieter Bruegel THE ELDER

DAMIAN HARVEY
Illustrated by TED SCANNA

978 1 4451 3315 7 pb
978 1 4451 3318 8 ebook

ELIZABETH I

DAMIAN HARVEY
Illustrated by RUPERT VAN WYK

978 1 4451 3302 7 pb
978 1 4451 3303 4 ebook

VICTORIA

DAMIAN HARVEY
Illustrated by RUPERT VAN WYK

978 1 4451 3314 0 pb
978 1 4451 3309 6 ebook

Tim BERNERS-LEE

DAMIAN HARVEY
Illustrated by JUDE DRWAN

978 1 4451 3322 5 pb
978 1 4451 3323 2 ebook

William CAXTON

DAMIAN HARVEY
Illustrated by JUDE DRWAN

978 1 4451 3312 6 pb
978 1 4451 3321 8 ebook